AROMATHERAPY

ALTERNATIVE HEALTH

AROMATHERAPY

GILL MARTIN

ILLUSTRATED BY SHAUN WILLIAMS

AN OPTIMA BOOK

© Gill Martin 1989

First published in 1989 by Macdonald Optima
This edition published in 1992 by Optima, a division of Little, Brown
and Company

British Library Cataloguing in Publication Data
Martin, Gill.
    Aromatherapy.
    1. Medicine. Natural remedies: Aromatic
    plant essential oils.
    I. Title   II. Series
    615'.32

    ISBN 0-356-21006-5

Little, Brown and Company (UK) Limited
165 Great Dover Street, London SE1 4YA

Printed in England by Clays Ltd, St Ives plc

Cover photograph by ZEFA — Harold Harris
Aromatherapy oils supplied by Life Works,
11 Southampton Road, London NW5

CONTENTS

1.
WHAT IS AROMATHERAPY?

Aromatherapy is a therapeutic treatment combining massage and essential oils to enhance well-being, restore balance and treat a variety of conditions. It is a natural method of healing with the pure aromatic substances and the nurturing touch of the therapist encouraging the body's own healing powers.

ANCIENT ORIGINS

Although the word 'aromatherapy' was not used until the beginning of this century, the use of aromatic plants is as old as human life. Our ancient ancestors soon discovered which would aid digestion, which would cure diarrhoea and used the plants around them to treat various health problems. Their sense of smell was probably more acute than ours; it was vital when hunting or avoiding the enemy and had not been deadened by the polluted atmosphere of today. They would use this when choosing plants, though the scent would be more noticeable when aromatic substances were burned, either when cooking food or when used as firewood. Through burning plants other properties were also discovered. The smoke might make the whole group feel sleepy or full of life and often special powers would be attributed to a particular herb. Burning plants became associated with rituals and magic, indeed 'smoking' was used to drive out evil spirits.

THE SMOKE MIGHT MAKE THE WHOLE GROUP FEEL FULL OF LIFE..

The use of aromatics also played an important part in the ancient civilizations of Egypt, Babylon, Greece and Rome. Though advanced in many ways, none of these peoples are thought to have developed a way of distilling the essential oils from the various herbs, trees and flowers. Most of the oils they used were infusions of fragrant substances in fatty oils, most notably in castor oil in Egypt and olive oil in Greece.

These ointments and oils were used for both medicinal and cosmetic purposes. On uncovering tombs in the pyramids, archaeologists have found various pots and jars made of alabaster or glass containing unguents still smelling of frankincense and myrrh, while clay tablets show how cedarwood oil was used for mummification as well as in hair and body

preparations. The ancient Greeks made use of the
medical knowledge of the Egyptians as well as making
their own discoveries about aromatic plants. In turn
the Greeks passed on much of their expertise to the
Romans.

In the West we are only just beginning to rediscover
the value of natural medicine, but in India and China
there is an unbroken tradition dating back to before
2,000 BC. In India, ancient origins form the basis of
the Ayurvedic medicine used today, while in China
herbal medicine and acupuncture have run side by side
since the days of the Yellow Emperor around 2,500 BC.

FIRST DISTILLATIONS OF ESSENTIAL OILS

Through the translation of Greek and Roman books,
medical knowledge built up over thousands of years
passed to the Arab world. It was here that essential
oils were first distilled towards the end of the tenth
century AD. The discovery of a method of distillation
which has changed very little even today, is attributed
to a physician known as Avicenna. The first essential
oil to be obtained this way was oil of rose and records
show that lavender, camomile and camphor oils were
also in use.

Back in Europe little is known of the progress of
herbal medicine during what is known historically as
the Dark Ages. It wasn't until the twelfth century that
we know crusading knights began to bring back
essences from Arabia. They also learnt the methods of
production and so soon essences from native plants
such as lavender, rosemary and basil were added to the
precious flower oils such as rose and jasmin. The use of
herbs and essential oils began to flourish. The
knowledge was made widely available in the form of
famous herbals such as those by Gerarde and Culpeper.
Posies of aromatic plants were used to ward off
infection, rooms were strewn with herbs and large

households even had their own stills for the production of essential oils.

The use of essential oils continued throughout the seventeenth and eighteenth centuries, mainly now by ordinary people in the home using skills passed on from generation to generation. A few essential oils such as peppermint, clove, lavender and camphor can still be found in pharmacopiea of today, though many others fell out of use as modern medicine developed.

Until the early twentieth century, essential oils had always been classed along with herbal remedies or valued for their cosmetic use. In the early 1920s Renée Gattefossé, a chemist in a French perfume company, became interested in and did much research into the medicinal properties of essential oils. There is a famous story of how on burning his hand he plunged it into neat lavender oil and to his surprise not only did the wound heal amazingly quickly but it also left no scarring. His book *Aromatherapie* was published in 1928.

The pioneers of aromatherapy came in the main part from France. Following Gattefossé came Dr Jean Valnet, a French army surgeon who used essential oils extensively during the French Indo-China war in treating battle wounds. He also undertook work in psychiatric hospitals using the oils with mentally disturbed patients. His book *Aromatherapie* published in 1964 is available in translation as *The Practice of Aromatherapy*. It is the classic text book for all serious practitioners of aromatherapy.

Around the same time as Dr Valnet, Mme Marguerite Maury was taking a different line of approach in her work with essential oils. She was a biochemist not a doctor, and used the oils externally for therapeutic and cosmetic purposes. She developed the basis of a therapy using a combination of essential oils and massage, a tradition carried on by many aromatherapists today.

The interest in aromatherapy in Britain is fairly

recent. Towards the end of her life Mme Maury moved to England and two of her assistants still have well known practices in London. In 1977 the first English work on aromatherapy, *The Art of Aromatherapy* by Robert Tisserand, was published. In the last ten years or so the therapy has begun to flourish, with many training schools and qualified therapists, and 1986 saw the formation of the International Federation of Aromatherapists, a national body for qualified aromatherapists.

NATURAL VERSUS SYNTHETIC

The essential oils used in aromatherapy are pure, natural substances which do not produce side-effects and are non-habit forming. Unfortunately this cannot always be said about conventional medicine. Though essential oils are simple substances in terms of their molecular structure, they are complex in terms of the number of active constituents that make up each

particular essence (see Chapter 2). As in any holistic therapy the maxim 'The whole is greater than the sum of the constituent parts' applies to aromatherapy.

When our ancestors used aromatic plants, their healing properties were put down to magic qualities. It wasn't until the nineteenth century that experimental chemists began looking in depth at various medicinal plants and succeeded in isolating their therapeutically active substances. Soon these isolated constituents began to be used in preference to the whole, natural plant or essence. Shortly after, towards the end of the nineteenth century, they were being produced synthetically in the laboratory and natural medicines fell out of use in favour of these new, modern drugs. Today the range of synthetic drugs is vast, with the major pharmaceutical companies trying to win over the consumer with their latest headache cure, or to convince doctors that their products are better than those of their rivals.

Medical science maintains that if the chemical formula of a synthetic drug is similar to that of a natural one then the body will accept it in the same way. In the aromatherapists' view this is not the case. With a natural substance, the body recognizes it as friendly, will use what it needs and pass the rest away. An artificial drug, however, will be identified as foreign and treated in the same way as invading bacteria. Over millions of years our bodies have adapted to the natural food and medicines found around us. It is too short a time to expect them to adapt to synthetic drugs and chemical food additives. So though a particular drug may be effective in treating a condition, it may also produce side-effects as the body tries hard to detoxify itself.

Side-effects in modern medicines are also the result of using isolated active constituents rather than the whole plant. An essential oil will contain a large number of principles which balance and enhance each other. Chemists may take one constituent and use it alone to treat a particular symptom, yet without the other parts of the plant the balance is lost and unwanted side-effects can occur.

DRUG DEPENDENCY

A further problem of chemically synthesized drugs is that the body will become habituated to them. At first one sleeping pill will have the desired effect, then as the body gets used to that two will be necessary. Similarly, with long-term use of laxatives the bowels lose their ability to function naturally.

One of the most common examples of drug dependency is the use of tranquillizers and anti-depressants. The body responds to these as it would to nicotine, caffeine or heroin and the taker becomes addicted. Severe withdrawal symptoms can occur and it is usually the people who resorted to tranquillizers in the first place who are least able to cope with them. Thus the body can become addicted to a substance whose effects are diminishing, so the dose is increased and the vicious circle completed.

TREATING THE WHOLE PERSON

Surrounded by such an array of medication, it is now the norm to run for the aspirin bottle at the first sign of a cold or headache. Similarly many people are not happy if they leave the doctor's surgery without a prescription. However, immediately removing the symptoms doesn't lead us to the original cause of the complaint. A headache may have many causes – tension in the neck, lack of sleep, a hangover. Removing the pain may allow us to carry on when the body is trying to tell us to rest. With a hangover the body is telling us it didn't like what we did to it and needs time to remove its toxins, not to be given more.

We often catch a cold when we're feeling run down and need a rest but instead of doing so we pump ourselves with chemicals and carry on. In the end the cold lasts a lot longer and leaves us feeling even more drained. Tranquillizers and anti-depressants may help in the short term but the problem causing the anxiety or depression will still be there.

When working with a client, an aromatherapist will not just treat a symptom but look for the possible causes. He or she will also look at the whole person.

WE OFTEN CATCH A COLD WHEN WE'RE FEELING RUN DOWN AND NEED A REST BUT INSTEAD OF DOING SO WE PUMP OURSELVES FULL OF CHEMICALS AND CARRY ON.

THE ROLE OF THE AROMATHERAPIST

Having seen some of the drawbacks of modern medicine, it is necessary at this point to say that the aromatherapist does not claim to be able to perform all the functions of a fully trained doctor. Though there is little doubt that essential oils can, for example, be more effective in fighting infection than antibiotics, the use of plant essences for serious conditions is limited either to herbalists or aromatherapists with a strong medical training (see Chapter 7). The majority of aromatherapists deal with non life-threatening conditions – minor ailments, skin problems and in particular stress or emotional difficulties. A client with more serious problems will be referred to a doctor, herbalist or homeopath depending on preference. Aromatherapy is a valuable preventative therapy which, by keeping a client well balanced emotionally and physically, reduces the chances of serious illness occurring.

A further distinction needs to be made between a trained aromatherapist and a beauty therapist using products with essential oils. The latter may advertise aromatherapy treatment but will often use a ready blended oil to treat a particular condition, without looking at the whole person. Though it is good to see a return to the use of natural ingredients, including essential oils, in cosmetics and beauty products, it is also necessary to see the broader scope of aromatherapy as a holistic treatment.

2.
HOW DOES AROMATHERAPY WORK?

The main tools of the aromatherapist are essential oils, and before explaining how they work it is necessary to know what they are and where they come from.

WHAT ARE ESSENTIAL OILS?

Essential oils are pure aromatic substances extracted or distilled from flowers, trees, fruits and herbs. They contain all the special properties of the plant including its odour. They are often thought of as being the life-force of the plant, the part of the plant which sums up the whole. The properties of the plant are not lost in the extraction process but in some way are concentrated and even enhanced. Thus essential oils are very powerful and need only be used in very small quantities. Essential oils are not fatty, some are very light and more like alcohol, a substance in which the oils will dissolve. They vary considerably in odour intensity and the rate at which they evaporate. Many are extremely volatile and they are usually stored in dark glass air-tight bottles to avoid deterioration.

All parts of a plant can be used to obtain essential oil, and in some cases different parts of the same plant produce different essences. From the orange tree, for example, we get orange oil from the rind of the fruit, petitgrain from the leaves and neroli from the blossom. The therapeutic value of each of these oils is different.

HOW ESSENTIAL OILS ARE EXTRACTED

Coming as they do from a range of different plants, fruits and flowers essential oils are extracted in a variety of different ways. Aromatic plants produce oils in special cells. These may be near the surface or within the secretory glands or ducts. Different plants also produce different quantities of oil and these two factors determine the method and ease of extraction as well as the amount of essential oil obtained.

The easiest method of extraction is by *simple pressure*, which is confined to the citrus fruit family. Orange, lemon, grapefruit, mandarin and bergamot are among those used in aromatherapy. The best quality oils are obtained by hand pressure though now most manufacturers use machines.

The most common method of extracting essential oils used today is *steam distillation*, a method familiar to most of us from our school chemistry days. The plant is held over boiling water and the steam produced draws off the essential oil. The steam is collected and cooled forming water in which the essential oil will either float or sink depending on its density. The water is then drawn off leaving only the essential oil. This oil from the *first* distillation is the best quality. The water can be re-used several times producing second, third and even fourth distillations. Essences obtained by this method include many of the commonly used ones such as lavender, rosemary, clary sage and peppermint. A

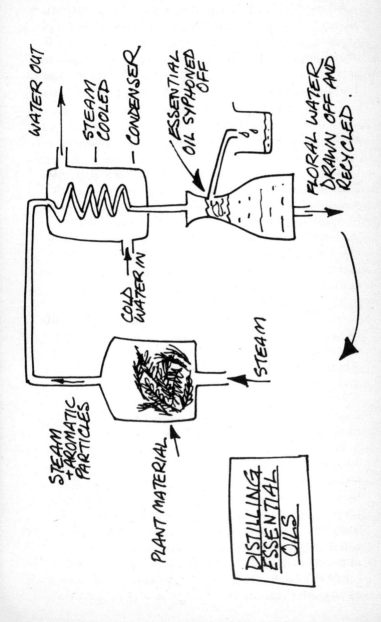

WATER OUT

STEAM COOLED

CONDENSER

ESSENTIAL OIL SYPHONED OFF

FLORAL WATER DRAWN OFF AND RECYCLED.

COLD WATER IN

STEAM

STEAM + AROMATIC PARTICLES

PLANT MATERIAL

DISTILLING ESSENTIAL OILS

cruder method of distillation involves heating the plant in water instead of above steam, producing an inferior quality oil. It is also possible to carry out the process in a vacuum where steam will be produced at a lower temperature, giving an even finer oil.

Some of the flower oils are extracted by a more complex process known as *enfleurage*. The flower heads are pressed in layers of purified fat and left until the essential oil has been removed and absorbed by the fat. As the flowers wilt they are replaced by new ones, this continuing until the fat is saturated with essential oil. This fatty compound is known as a *pommade* and was often used as an ointment or perfume. Now it is more common to continue the process and remove the essential oil from the fat. This is done by mixing the pommade with alcohol, in which the essential oil dissolves but the fat is insoluble. The alcohol is then evaporated off by gentle heating, leaving the pure essential oil in the container. Oils obtained in this way are known as *absolutes*. The flowers which yield these absolutes contain very little oil so vast quantities are needed. It takes about eight million jasmin flowers to produce one kilogramme of essential oil of jasmin. These have to be hand picked at night as the odour is most intense after dark, and also before the flowers are a day old. This explains the extremely high cost of the jasmin absolute. Fortunately absolutes tend to be even more concentrated in both odour and therapeutic value than essential oils and so only very small quantities are needed.

Some flowers now have their oil removed by means of an *organic solvent*. This is a complicated process which involves mixing the flowers in solvent to extract the oil, then via various stages of heating, cooling and filtering, alcohol is added to dissolve the oil. The alcohol is then evaporated off as described above. The flower oils produced by this method are not as fine a quality as the absolutes but the production costs are considerably less.

PURITY OF ESSENTIAL OILS

Essential oils are now becoming more widely available and there is a dazzling array of different producers, packaging and prices. For the lay person, knowing which ones to buy can be quite a problem. Most serious aromatherapists will buy their oils direct from suppliers by mail order, or in specialist shops. After working with the oils for a while the therapist develops a sensitivity towards them and is able to perceive differences between different bottles of the same essential oil. No two bottles of marjoram, for example, will smell the same. The aroma will not only depend on purity but also on where the aromatic plant grew when it was harvested and what the weather had been like. The same essential oil from the same supplier may smell quite different from year to year.

There are, however, a few guidelines to follow when buying essential oils. The first is price. Unfortunately if the oils seem cheap in comparison to other suppliers then the quality won't be as good. There simply aren't short cuts to producing good quality essential oils. Cheaper oils may be from third or fourth distillations or they may be from the wrong part of the plant. For example the best quality oil from the juniper tree is from the juniper berry. An oil produced from the leaves as well will be cheaper, but not so powerful in its therapeutic properties. The oils may also have been mixed with cheaper oils or in some cases even with synthetic oils to stretch them further. A classic example is the fact that France actually exports more lavender oil than it produces. It is usually at the level of the manufacturer or exporter that this adulteration takes place so the wholesaler or retailer may be unaware of it. This is why most serious therapists use established suppliers who know the business well and can offer a guarantee of purity.

Another point to watch for is a uniform price throughout one manufacturer's range. Due to different methods of extraction the prices of different essential oils should vary enormously. If they don't, you will either be paying over the odds for your orange oil or be buying an inferior quality sandalwood. Also make sure the oils are packaged in dark glass bottles. The effects of light will cause deterioration of the oils, so clear glass bottles are no good and plastic is even worse as the oils can attack the plastic causing contamination. Also check that the oils have not already been diluted with a vegetable oil such as soya oil, as some suppliers do.

There is a list of reputable suppliers at the back of the book, but if you discover others then spend some time talking to the stockist about them. If they know a lot about the oils and can tell you about their suppliers then, unless they are very unscrupulous, the oils will probably be all right to buy.

CHEMISTRY AND STRUCTURE OF ESSENTIAL OILS

Plants manufacture essential oils by breaking down naturally occurring elements such as carbon, oxygen and nitrogen and putting them together in different combinations to produce aromatic molecules. From a relatively small number of building blocks put together in different ways, a large number of different essential oils are produced.

The constituents of essential oils are mostly based on a framework of carbon atoms made up in multiples of five. Onto this framework will hang atoms of other elements, producing a wide range of different aromatic molecules. These molecules are small, normally consisting of chains of around 25 or 30 carbon atoms with associated elements hanging on. This molecular simplicity is of great importance when considering how the body can absorb the oils. Other compounds may consist of chains of many thousands of atoms.

These different compounds can be put into a variety of groups such as acids, alcohol, phenols or terpenes. It is these constituents that the chemists separate and use individually. Phenols, such as eugenol and eucalyptol, are powerful antiseptics yet it has been shown that using the whole oil is more effective. A 1 per cent dilution of clove oil is three or four times more effective than its main constituent eugenol. Again we have another example of synergy, that is the co-ordination of various constituents being more active than just one part.

It is the combination of many active constituents that makes each oil unique. It also accounts for the fact that one essential oil may have a wide range of uses and also that many different oils can be used for the same condition. This often produces a certain amount of scepticism in the lay person – can one oil really treat such a variety of symptoms? Taking lavender as an example, it can be used as a pain reliever, a decongestant, a disinfectant or an anti-depressant to name just a few uses. It can be used for complaints as diverse as acne, migraine, 'flu and insomnia. Similarly a person suffering from migraine may equally well be treated using marjoram or for 'flu, tea-tree may be used. It is by working holistically that the aromatherapist will pick the right combination of oils for a particular person at a particular time.

In summary, essential oils are simple in terms of their molecular structure, yet complex in the number of active constituents which make up each individual essence. It is the combination of these constituents which give the essential oil its own distinctive aroma and range of therapeutic values. This combination will also prove more effective than any one isolated component.

HOW THE BODY USES ESSENTIAL OILS

The challenge most often levelled at aromatherapy by the sceptic is 'how can just smelling something do you any good?'. There is, of course, far more to aromatherapy than that but nevertheless our sense of smell does play an important part. Today, smell is probably our most neglected sense, though to our ancestors it was a vital part of their defence mechanism. They would use it when tracking animals for food or to sense that they themselves were being hunted. Indeed our reaction to smell is actually quicker than to pain or sound.

SMELL WAS A VITAL PART OF OUR ANCESTORS' DEFENCE MECHANISM...

In some way or another we cultivate our other senses. We watch television or visit an art gallery, we listen to music, we go out for a meal and we may stroke a cat or touch our partners. How often do we actually do something for the sense of smell alone? We might remark upon smells when we sense them, that of

new baked bread or fresh mown hay, but only rarely do
we bend down to a rose simply to enjoy its fragrance.
Even perfume is often just sprayed on as the last stage
in our grooming routine.

Our sense of smell, however, is more powerful than
we think. In fact when we eat that meal, it is our noses
which really reveal how good it 'tastes'. Our taste buds
can only distinguish between salty, sweet, bitter and
sour, while our sense of smell is ten thousand times
more sensitive. We all come across this when we have
a cold and food seems tasteless. When smokers give up
cigarettes one of the first things they notice is how food
tastes much better and how their sense of smell has
improved. In fact, pollution has an effect on our ability
to smell. Drive out of London or any other big city to
the coast and everything smells so much better; food on
a picnic always tastes better than it does at home. So
our sense of smell is actually at work though we don't
realize it. This is just one way in which our olfactory
system is working for us. Think about what happens
when we smell food cooking, how it makes us feel
hungry, or how the smell of rotten food can make us
feel sick. How often does a particular smell remind us
of some past event? The perfume industry bases its
marketing strategy on suggesting that a perfume will
create a certain mood or that an aftershave will act as
an aphrodisiac. Somehow our sense of smell is linked
with a variety of things from memory to sexual arousal
to digestion.

HOW THE OLFACTORY SYSTEM WORKS

Just behind the bridge of the nose is a structure called
the olfactory bulb and from here the olfactory nerve
cells reach down into the mucus of the nasal cavity.
Extending from these nerve cells are tiny hairs known
as cilia, which are excited in response to olfactory
stimuli (or things that smell). This impulse passes

through the nerve cells to the olfactory bulb which in turn sends the impulse directly to the brain via the olfactory tracts. The olfactory nerve tracts run into the part of the brain known as the limbic system. It is this part of the brain that is in someway tied up with memory and emotion. In addition to this, the limbic system is connected to the hypothalamus. This structure governs the pituitary gland which in turn controls the other glands and therefore our whole hormonal system. So when we smell something there is an immediate effect on our autonomic nervous system and our hormonal system. These systems are responsible for fear and anger responses, appetite control, growth rate, sexual responses, digestion, heart rate, our reaction to stress, memory and many other responses. This not only demonstrates how important our sense of smell is but illustrates how powerful aromatherapy can be in helping with emotional problems.

We may also react to smells in an unconscious way. At present work is being done to find out more about

AT PRESENT WORK IS BEING DONE TO FIND OUT MORE ABOUT PHEROMONES...

pheromones, or odorous substances produced by the sebaceous glands of humans. Pheromones are complex substances which are thought to have an effect on those around us. They tend to be produced under the arms and around the genitals and the glands excrete more pheromones when we are frightened, excited or sexually aroused. Thus they are thought to play a part in the way people are attracted to one another or the way we can sense each other's emotions.

ABSORPTION INTO THE BLOODSTREAM

Our olfactory system is not the only one activated when we smell something, such as an essential oil. The aromatic molecules will have evaporated into the air and can be taken down into the lungs along with the air we breathe. Some will be exhaled in the next breath, but some will pass to the bloodstream in the same way as oxygen and nutrients are transported around the body. Blood circulates around the body very rapidly indeed and so oils taken in by this means can have an effect in a short space of time. Some oils have a general effect on the whole body while others have a special affinity for a particular organ. On reaching this organ some or all of the essential oil will be deposited. When it has used all it needs then the organ will excrete what is left. So for example an oil used by the kidneys will be excreted in the urine while an oil used by the stomach will pass out via the digestive system. Thus the oils will pass safely through the body being used as the body needs them.

The second way of getting essential oils into the bloodstream is via the skin. Essential oils can be mixed with natural vegetable oils, creams or lotions and applied locally or over the whole body. If the molecular structure of a substance is small enough then it will be absorbed by the skin. The molecular size is of great importance in this process. As stated earlier, essential oils are of very small molecular size and so it is important that any carrier oil they are mixed in must have small molecules too. Mineral-based oils such as Vaseline or baby oil, or products containing animal fats such as lanolin will not penetrate the skin but sit on the surface clogging the pores.

Once the oils have passed through the skin they will be absorbed by tissue fluids, taken into the lymphatic system and from there will pass into the bloodstream to be circulated around the body. The time this takes varies from person to person, anything from around 20 minutes to several hours. Likewise the effects may last from several hours up to several days.

A third way for an essential oil to reach the bloodstream is via the digestive system. This process of absorption takes longer than by any other method as the oils pass, along with food matter, through the complex workings of the digestive system. There is a split amongst aromatherapists as to whether essential oils should ever be taken internally, as not only is transcutaneous absorption (through the skin) safer, it can also be a lot quicker (see Chapter 3).

So there are various methods by which the body receives essential oils, all varying in speed. Whichever method we use we always smell the aroma and some of the aromatic particles are always inhaled. Thus, for example, when a blend of oils is massaged into the body there is the instantaneous effect on the olfactory system and the rapid absorption through the lungs, followed by the slightly slower absorption through the skin.

HEALTHY CELLS – HEALTHY BODY

Once in the bloodstream, how does an essential oil have an effect on the body? To take an example, essential oil of rosemary has an affinity with the liver. On reaching the liver in its journey through the bloodstream, the essential oil needed will be dissolved into the tissue fluid, along with any other substances the liver needs such as oxygen and the fat-soluble vitamins. The essential oil contains a number of chemical substances that the liver cells might need to remain healthy. These simple substances can be used easily and therefore rapidly. Other organs will use the essential oil in a similar way.

Some oils, however, are less specific in their effect and act on body tissues in general. They may perform a variety of functions – stimulating, cleansing and generally toning. Their most important function is their ability to balance the body systems and improve the body's own defence mechanisms. Essential oils will also help promote healthy new cell growth; in particular neroli (orange blossom) and lavender are noted for this. Some essential oils also contain plant hormones which can either stimulate or balance the production of our hormones. Fennel for example contains oestrogen.

It is because essential oils are recognized as friendly by the body that they are so readily accepted by the cells. And a healthy body depends on healthy cells.

3.
WHAT THE AROMATHERAPIST DOES

There are various ways in which the aromatherapist can use his or her basic tools, the essential oils, in treating a patient. In general a session will be centred around a massage but in some cases other methods of administering the oils will be used or advised for use at home.

INHALATIONS

Though this method could be used with any oil for any complaint, as a way of getting oil into the bloodstream, it is usually used for problems of the lungs or air passages. The aromatherapist will most likely suggest inhalations at home to back up the treatment, but sometimes they might be appropriate during a treatment session. This could be the case with a patient suffering from sinusitis where the condition is advanced and painful. An inhalation may help to loosen the trapped fluid and the antibiotic properties of the oils will help to fight the infection. This could be followed by a gentle face massage to encourage drainage and ease a headache if there is one.

An inhalation is carried out by adding a few drops of essential oil to near boiling water in a bowl. The client leans over the bowl with a towel over his or her head and takes deep breaths. Breathing through the nose will help to unblock nasal passages while breathing through the mouth will ease a sore throat. The steam in itself helps to fight infection and with the antibiotic and antiviral properties of essential oils, inhalations make an effective way of fighting a cold or 'flu. The amount of time spent over the water starts with short bursts of about 30 seconds, building up to several minutes as the client feels more comfortable. Lavender is a good oil for colds and can also be used to ensure a good night's sleep. Some of the oils commonly associated with the treatment of colds, such as eucalyptus or thyme, are more stimulating and best avoided in the evening. Bronchitis sufferers can also benefit from inhalations. Any phlegm will be loosened and then a gentle massage will be comforting and help ease any tension caused by the strain of coughing. For some skin complaints a similar method is used to

YOUR MUM SHY OR WHAT?

steam the face. In conditions such as acne where massage may be painful, after thorough cleansing of the skin a steam facial may be used instead. Some therapists use a facial steamer for this purpose instead of the rather crude method involving bowls and boiling water.

COMPRESSES

An aromatic compress comprises a clean cloth soaked in either hot or cold water to which essential oils have been added. The excess water is wrung out and the cloth applied repeatedly to the affected area. An aromatherapist may use a compress where massage is contra-indicated or uncomfortable for the client. Recent injuries such as sprains, torn muscles or bruises should not be massaged, but relief can be felt using compresses. A cold compress containing analgesic oils such as lavender and camomile will help relieve pain and reduce swelling. Some headaches respond better to cold than heat and where massage is uncomfortable, a cold compress with oils such as lavender and peppermint may help. Hot compresses can be used for chronic conditions such as rheumatism or fibrositis and persistent pain from old injuries. Menstrual cramp responds well to hot compresses of marjoram oil and the same can be used for headaches if they stem from tension at the back of the neck. A further technique is to use alternate hot and cold compresses, an old naturopathic technique which is said to help the healing of old injuries.

BATHS

Though obviously not a part of the session, an aromatherapist will often advise aromatic baths as a back-up treatment between sessions. He or she will make up a blend of oils, ready diluted in a carrier oil for the client to use either in the morning or evening. A long soak in a warm bath before going to bed can be soothing and relaxing and, with oils such as lavender and marjoram, particularly helpful for insomnia sufferers. If your problem is getting going in the morning then a bath first thing with stimulating oils such as rosemary would be advised for you.

VAPORIZATION

Evaporating essential oils into the atmosphere can be useful either for creating a mood or fighting infection. Many aromatherapists use an oil burner in their treatment rooms before a client arrives. This can be very helpful for anxious or nervous people to help them relax before they have a massage. At home they can be used for a similar purpose – maybe the whole family would benefit from a calming, relaxing fragrance. Some essential oils, namely eucalyptus and tea-tree, contain constituents which are air-borne bacteriacides, so can be extremely useful during epidemics of 'flu, chickenpox or measles. They also make good insect repellants and room fresheners. You can buy specially made vaporizers consisting of a container holding a candle, supporting a dish to which water and a few drops of essential oil have been added. The candle gently warms the water and oil, which evaporate producing a wonderful aroma. Other simpler methods include putting the oils into a bowl of boiling water, placing a damp cloth containing essential oils over a radiator or putting a few drops of essential oil on a light bulb before switching it on.

INTERNAL MEDICATION

Aromatherapists can really be divided into two groups:

those who advocate the use of essential oils as an internal medication and those who don't. These two different schools of thought can really be traced back to two of the pioneers of modern day aromatherapy, Dr Jean Valnet and Mme Marguerite Maury. Jean Valnet was a qualified doctor and surgeon and one of his main interests was in the antibacterial effects of the essential oils. Oils were used internally and externally as appropriate. Mme Maury on the other hand had no medical qualifications. She was a biochemist whose interest was in the cosmetic use of the oils and their effect on mood and emotion. She concentrated entirely on the external application of essential oils, never using them as an internal medication. Thus there is a clear difference in backgrounds. Many aromatherapists in Britain do not have previous medical backgrounds (though all those who are members of the International Federation of Aromatherapists have followed a course in anatomy and physiology) and prefer to stick to the external use of the oils, with massage being an equally important part of the therapy.

Many aromatherapists are beginning to see that in many ways transcutaneous absorption (through the skin) can be more powerful than ingestion and also safer. There are several reasons for this. Firstly, the skin is the largest organ of the body and tests have shown that if necessary more oil can be absorbed through the skin in a short space of time than could be tolerated by the stomach. Secondly, essential oils are very powerful substances and if used in large quantities internally they could irritate or damage the stomach lining. There is also the possibility of toxicity when they reach the liver and kidneys. It also takes longer for the essential oils to be distributed around the body when they have to go via the digestive system. Having said this, internal usage is practised with success by medically trained doctors using aromatherapy and also by some herbalists. Those aromatherapists who do use oils internally do so in small quantities which have been well diluted. Dilution is usually done in a small amount of alcohol which is then diluted further with water, so very small quantities of essential oil are being taken at a time. Some books suggest taking the oil on sugar or honey, a practice which is now frowned upon. The sugar does not dissolve the essential oil but just makes it more palatable.

The International Federation of Aromatherapists has a policy by which its members do not use essential oils internally in the treatment of clients. There is a move, however, to increase the medical use of essential oils in Britain (for more discussion see Chapter 7).

MASSAGE

Massage is an ancient healing art with an unfortunate reputation in modern society. Fortunately, it is now becoming accepted as a serious healing therapy and the variety of different types of massage grow in number all the time. Bio-dynamic massage, shiatsu, postural integration, rolfing and pulsing are all forms of massage but the practitioner's method of working is very different in each case.

Aromatherapy massage was developed as a means of applying oils to the skin, but the benefits far exceed the simple absorption of the oils into the body. Massage will help ease tight muscles, improve circulation and lymph flow, help the body eliminate toxins or help ease pain in a specific area. Our natural reaction to pain is to rub or hold the hurt area, a toe stubbed on a chair feels better if we hold and rub it. Massage is an extension of this natural reaction. Massage also has a powerful effect on the mind and emotions. It can help increase awareness of our own bodies, help balance the flow of energy or release emotional tension stored in our muscles. It also provides the means for direct contact between the aromatherapist and his or her client, helping to increase communication and build up trust.

Aromatherapy massage is a combination of techniques from other massage styles, adapted to help the absorption of the essential oils and to promote a feeling of well-being for the client. No two aromatherapists will massage in the same way, nor will one aromatherapist give the same massage to all clients or even give the same massage to one client on each visit. Each massage given is unique, tailored to the specific needs of that person at that time. Each aromatherapist develops his or her own style, which will be constantly altered and adapted.

Despite the personal variations in technique, all aromatherapy massage will be smooth and flowing, without harsh or jarring movements. Stroking or *effleurage* is a movement from Swedish massage much used in aromatherapy. It consists of long, slow, gentle strokes made with the whole hand and normally directed towards the heart. The pressure can be varied, with deeper strokes affecting the muscles and circulation while lighter strokes tend to have more of an effect on the nervous system. Smooth but deeper kneading movements follow, to warm the muscles for any deeper work. At this point aromatherapy massage leaves Swedish massage and its more vigorous hacking and pounding movements – while being an excellent form of physical massage, most Swedish massage doesn't take into account the mental and emotional state of the receiver.

As a total reaction against this during the 1960s, intuitive massage became popular. The giver would 'tune in' to the receiver and use whatever touch and movement he or she felt appropriate. Though this was a wonderful way of heightening personal awareness and developing non-verbal communication, a less experienced masseur could easily miss areas of muscle spasm which needed attention. Today intuitive massage is less vague in its practice and it is now taught with various strokes to be used as and when needed.

Aromatherapy massage is based on a similar approach. The therapist aims to give the body what it needs on a physical level while still remaining nurturing and taking into account the emotional state of the receiver. Some people respond well to a fairly deep, physical massage while someone with emotional problems may need more gentle handling. Any deeper work on knotted muscles will be done gently rather than vigorously. This work can sometimes be painful and the therapist will decide just what is appropriate for each client. A small amount of discomfort might be felt in easing out a muscle spasm, but too high a degree of pain will cause the client to tense up, defeating the point of a massage. The aromatherapist will sense what a client needs, but will also ask if a massage feels alright and/or request to be told if it is too painful.

MIXING THE MASSAGE OILS

Essential oils are very concentrated substances and will always be mixed into a carrier oil for use during a massage. A maximum of 3 per cent essential oil is all that is needed, that is 3 drops in a 5ml teaspoon of base oil. The base oil can be any natural vegetable oil. Grapeseed is popular as it is light, odourless and very easily absorbed by the skin, though almond and sunflower are often used too. Richer oils, such as wheatgerm, avocado, apricot kernel and jojoba, may be added in small quantities for drier skins or for use on the face. The aromatherapist will usually make up the oil just before each massage though he or she may also make up a larger quantity for the client to take home.

BLENDING ESSENTIAL OILS

On each visit, the aromatherapist will make up a blend of essential oils especially suited to you at that particular time. They will be chosen for their therapeutic powers and their effects upon the nervous system, but whichever oils are chosen they must produce a harmonious aroma. However good a blend may seem from a therapeutic viewpoint, if it smells awful, it certainly won't be of much use! Just as an individual oil is more powerful than the sum of its constituents, so a blend can be more powerful than each essential oil on its own. The various oils will often subtly enhance each other in some way.

An aromatherapist will know through experience which oils work well together and which don't and will usually have favourite blends. That does not mean that he or she won't sometimes make mistakes! The possible combinations are limitless, leaving plenty of scope for experimentation. There are, however, certain theories about blending oils which are said to lead to a harmonious blend.

Firstly, there is blending according to notes. As in classic perfumery, essential oils are divided into groups of top notes, middle notes and bass notes. Top notes are the ones we smell first in a blend and are the lightest and most volatile oils. Next come the middle notes, followed by the bass notes which are heavier with a lingering aroma. In classic perfumery a mixture containing a top, middle and bass note will produce a well balanced blend. The quantities of each oil will not necessarily be the same as they vary a great deal in odour intensity. A very little amount of an oil such as camomile, for example, will overpower the others in a blend. This theory of blending does have its faults. To begin with, the experts don't always agree on which oils are top, middle and bass notes. Some oils will also change depending on the crop, season or where they were produced. Sometimes a blend still won't smell good even after these rules have been followed.

Blending by families is another way of mixing oils. These may either be botanical families or groups of oils from just trees or just herbs or just citrus fruits for example. Mixing oils from the same type or family of plants usually produces a pleasant blend. Sometimes combining families, such as citrus with spices, will work well. Some aromatherapists see oils in terms of colours. For example, an odour such as petitgrain (orange leaves) is green and fresh, whereas some marjorams are brown and earthy. Blending the colours may produce a harmonious blend. Indeed some therapists use colour healing, so the 'colour' of the oil will also have a therapeutic effect as well as the odour and chemical properties.

When the aromatherapist has mixed the blend, he or she will ask the client if they like it. The treatment won't be much good if the client finds the odour offensive. Sometimes the client will be asked which oil they prefer from a few different ones. There is a lot to be said for intuitive knowledge of what the body needs. The whole area of smell is highly subjective, but the experienced aromatherapist will be able to select a blend that is of therapeutic value and also has an aroma to suit each client.

4.
THINKING ABOUT AROMATHERAPY

Who goes to an aromatherapist? What do they do? How many sessions will I need? How do I find one? All these are questions people ask when thinking about aromatherapy, and in this chapter I'll attempt to answer these and others which might crop up.

Who goes to an aromatherapist?
Anyone and everyone, from babies to people in their nineties, can benefit. It is never too early or late to start aromatherapy. It is often a therapy which seems to appeal more to women than men, but both can benefit equally. You won't necessarily come out of the treatment room smelling like a perfume counter – aromas vary from the delicate floral types to the woody more 'masculine' smells.

What does an aromatherapist treat?
Medically qualified aromatherapists may choose to use essential oils to treat any condition, including serious

life-threatening conditions such as infectious diseases or even AIDS. However, the majority of aromatherapists have clients with problems of a less serious nature. Some of the conditions which respond well to aromatherapy include nervous complaints such as stress, anxiety, depression and tension – both mental and physical; skin problems including eczema and acne and menstrual problems including pre-menstrual tension. Rheumatism and arthritis sufferers can feel great relief from aromatherapy massage, usually combined with a change in diet. Circulatory disorders can be helped a great deal, as can respiratory problems. If your particular condition does not respond to the treatment, your aromatherapist will be able to refer you to another more suitable therapist – osteopath, homeopath, acupuncturist or other who may be able to help.

Essential oils can also be extremely effective in treating acute conditions, such as colds, sore throats, sinusitis, constipation, diarrhoea, headaches and migraine, conditions which are often treated at home by drugs bought over the counter at the chemist. With these drugs the symptoms clear up and the sufferer is happy until the condition recurs. In all these situations the problem is being supressed without its real causes being investigated. Though it is not always possible to see the aromatherapist when a problem actually arises, by visiting your therapist regularly, he or she can talk to you about any recurring problems and help you to build up your own aromatherapy first aid kit to treat minor conditions as they occur (see Chapter 6).

Do I need to be ill to see an aromatherapist?
The answer to this is most definitely 'no'. Almost everyone will benefit from having a more relaxed mind and body. Aromatherapy is a wonderful preventative form of treatment. Circulation will be improved, it will help clear the body of toxins and increase the body's

own potential to heal itself and fight off infection. Some people consider aromatherapy to be a luxurious treat, others feel it is an important part of their routine. Attitudes depend on whether we feel that having a well-balanced mind and body is something towards which we strive in order to weather the pressures of modern living or merely a pleasant interlude in a life normally full of stress and tension. Most of us lead a hectic life, whether we are dealing with vast sums of money on the stock exchange, coping with a home and young children, or these days perhaps both! It is important to stop once in a while and 'treat' ourselves to something that is just for us, something relaxing and nurturing. An aromatherapy session can provide that for everyone.

MOST OF US LEAD A HECTIC LIFE, WHETHER WE ARE DEALING WITH VAST SUMS OF MONEY ON THE STOCK EXCHANGE, COPING WITH A HOME AND YOUNG CHILDREN, OR PERHAPS BOTH!

How do I find a practitioner?
Aromatherapists work in a variety of places. Many have practices at home, others work in health clubs or

sports centres. A local natural health clinic is often a good place to try. If they don't have an aromatherapist on the premises, they will often be able to recommend one who works locally. Beware of beauty salons. Many of them advertise aromatherapy when they have beauty therapists using ready prepared essential oils. If in doubt ask about their qualifications (see below).

What qualifications should I look for?

There are many schools of aromatherapy around now, all giving their own diplomas. However, to be sure your aromatherapist has undergone a thorough training, look for the initials M.I.F.A. (Member of the International Federation of Aromatherapists). The Federation monitors the training courses and will only give membership to those who offer a good grounding in the use of essential oils and massage, as well as anatomy and physiology. They can also provide a list of qualified aromatherapists in your area.

Making an appointment

In most cases you will need to book an appointment in advance. People either visit the practice or book by phone. Most centres have receptionists who will book the appointment and may ask you about the nature of your complaint. If they do, just give a very brief description so the practitioner will know what to expect. If you do have to cancel an appointment for some reason, you may be asked to give notice, usually 24 hours, otherwise you may have to pay a cancellation fee.

How long will a session take?

This does vary between therapists, depending on how and where they work. In general the first session will be longer, usually 1½ hours, though sometimes it could be two. Subsequent sessions are usually an hour in length, though again this could vary depending on the practitioner and the nature of the complaint.

How often will I need to go?

Again this will depend on your own particular needs and the way your chosen therapist works. Though you are likely to feel good after one session, like any alternative therapy it is not an instant cure. In cases where the complaint has taken months or years to develop, it may take some time before any improvement is seen. Other cases may respond very quickly but regular visits to the aromatherapist will have great preventative value. Many people think of an aromatherapy session as a treat. While this may be true, living as we do in a highly stressful and hectic environment, it is important to allow ourselves time for something beneficial and nurturing on a regular basis. A regular aromatherapy session, be it weekly or monthly, can help us to keep our balance and prevent illness from occurring.

How much does a session cost?

Charges vary from place to place, but the average in Britain is around £15 to £20. Some practitioners may charge more for the longer initial session. Oils for home use are usually included in the cost of the treatment.

When should I book a first appointment?

Obviously it will be better if you haven't eaten a large meal just before the visit as this could cause discomfort during the massage. Similarly it would be unwise to come to a session after drinking alcohol. It is often a good idea to allow yourself some time to relax before and after a session, especially on the first visit. Arriving hot and flustered can make it difficult for you to relax very quickly or dashing back to work straight away will soon make you forget how you felt during the session. Perhaps try booking your first appointment in the late afternoon so you can go home and relax afterwards. Or if you're at home with children, try a session in the morning then allow yourself a bit of time to relax before they come home from school. On subsequent visits, when you know what to expect, you will probably be able to relax more easily at first and carry the benefits away with you in a calm manner.

Can I drive home afterwards?

It may seem like a silly question, but it is a good idea to tell the aromatherapist how you intend to get home. Some oils are extremely sedating and may impair your judgement for driving. You may be given some oils to take home for use later.

Do I have to take all my clothes off?

As essential oils are applied on the skin for absorption then you will need to take some clothes off. For a full massage you will usually be asked to take off everything, or if you prefer you can leave your pants on. You will be given a large towel and during the massage the therapist will keep covered the parts of the body he or she isn't working on. If however, you feel uncomfortable taking off all your clothes, then do tell the aromatherapist. One of the main aims is to create an atmosphere in which you can relax and feel comfortable. If at first this means you keep some clothes on then the aromatherapist will work on what parts of the body he or she can, until you feel happy about removing the rest of your clothes.

Bearing in mind that you will have to take most of your clothes off for the massage, it is a good idea not to wear lots of fiddly garments which take a long time to take off and put back on. This includes jewellery as you will be asked to remove this as well.

How should I prepare for the visit?

On the first visit the aromatherapist will take a full case history (see Chapter 5). It will be helpful for the therapist and easier for you if you spend a few minutes beforehand thinking about some of the things you might be asked. These will include your past medical history and that of your family, your present lifestyle and the particular reason for your visit. Be prepared to answer questions about your mental and emotional state as well. The aromatherapist isn't being nosey but needs to know all about you before making the choice of oils.

Should I tell my doctor?

If you are seeing a doctor for any particular complaint or if you are taking a course of prescribed drugs then it is a good idea to tell him or her that you are planning to see an aromatherapist. The reaction may vary a great deal from highly sceptical to positively encouraging. However, whatever their opinion of

A BUSY GP WILL NOT HAVE TIME TO DEVOTE AN HOUR TO EACH PATIENT TO LISTEN AND ENCOURAGE...

essential oils, most doctors do recognize the benefits of regular massage. There is sometimes a great deal of antagonism between orthodox and alternative healthcare practitioners and we can do a lot to relieve this by actually talking to each other and complementing each other's skills. A busy general practitioner will not have time to devote an hour to each patient to listen and encourage them, so may be only too pleased to have someone else do this. Likewise the aromatherapist will value the doctor's diagnostic skills which will help in the choice of treatment. If you communicate between your two practitioners there should be no need for any problems.

Can I see other alternative practitioners as well?
As with your family doctor, if you are seeing any other alternative practitioners, then it is a good idea to tell them that you are going to an aromatherapist as well. Indeed some may even refer you to one, especially in a clinic where many different practitioners work together. If, for example, you are seeing an osteopath, once he is sure that he's corrected any structural problems, he may advise regular massage to keep you in good shape. Osteopathy can be a fairly mechanical process, seeing an aromatherapist may help with the emotional side of the problem. Or perhaps you are seeing a homeopath or herbalist. These therapies will deal with both physical and emotional problems but don't involve any body contact, so again massage could fill in this side of things. If you are seeing a homeopath, it is especially important to tell him or her before you see the aromatherapist, as some essential oils may antidote the homeopathic remedies. Your homeopath may be able to write a note for the aromatherapist so that he or she knows which oils to avoid.

On the other hand, an aromatherapist may recommend that you see another alternative practitioner as well. If your back problem, for example, has not improved after a few sessions then the aromatherapist may ask you to see an osteopath for a second opinion. Or if the massage and essential oils bring up a lot of emotional problems or confusions, then some form of psychotherapy could be of great value. The main concern of any healthcare practitioner is your well-being, so they will work together however they can to find the best treatment for you.

5.
THE FIRST VISIT

Having decided to have your first aromatherapy session, you might feel a little apprehensive when you arrive at the clinic or practitioner's home. Don't worry. Everything will be done to make you feel at ease. The health centre where I have my practice has a receptionist who will tell you what to do and a pleasant relaxing waiting room, always full of flowers and books and magazines on natural therapies and healthy living. The treatment rooms are clean and fresh looking, without the clinical appearance of many doctors' surgeries or dentists' waiting rooms. If the aromatherapist works from home, he or she will probably take you straight to the treatment room which will be furnished in soft relaxing colours. The main focus of the room will be the massage couch. Then there will be all the bottles of essential oils, base oils, creams and dishes and a pile of soft towels. This is of course a generalization, but there will be a genuine attempt to make you feel relaxed.

After taking off your coat, you will be asked to sit down, ready for the case history. The therapist may have a desk but often a couple of chairs are used to create a less formal atmosphere.

THE CASE HISTORY

The initial case history is an important part of your
aromatherapy treatment. It will give the therapist
details of your present condition and your lifestyle in
general so he or she can choose a blend of oils
especially for you.

To begin with you will be told a bit about
aromatherapy and how the therapist works as an
individual and also exactly what he or she will do
during the session. Then your therapist will start your
case history. Some aromatherapists will use printed
sheets, others just a note pad. Don't be put off by this
note taking, the aromatherapist needs to keep a
detailed record for future use. After asking basic facts
like name, address, date of birth, family status and
occupation he or she will ask about the reason for the
visit. This could be for a specific complaint or for
relaxation or perhaps just curiosity.

If you have come about a specific condition then the
aromatherapist will want to know as much as possible
about it. You will be asked when it started and if
anything else significant happened in your life at the
same time. The aromatherapist will want to know
what makes the condition better and what makes it
worse. On a physical level, you will be asked to try to
describe any pain or other symptoms, while on an
emotional level you will be asked how you cope with
the condition or even how your family cope with it. It
is useful to have thought about some of these things
beforehand. It is not easy to put such things as pain
into words, but it will help the therapist greatly.

Previous medical history
As well as your present state of health, the
aromatherapist will need to know about your past
medical history. This will help in working out any
underlying causes of a present condition and will also

point out essential oils which should be avoided or any contra-indications to massage. For example, a recent operation or accident may mean modifying the massage to account for this. Or if you have ever suffered from epilepsy, then certain essential oils must be avoided. It is important for the aromatherapist to know about illnesses such as allergies, diabetes or heart conditions. You will also be asked about the medical history of members of your family, as there may be a predisposition toward certain illnesses which runs within the family. The aromatherapist will also want to know of any medication you have been prescribed in the past or are taking at present. Most women forget to mention the contraceptive pill, but it can be important to know.

Your body
Returning to the present, the aromatherapist will enquire about the vital functions of the body such as the digestive, respiratory and menstrual systems. You will be asked about any problems to do with digestion or bowel movements and perhaps about your appetite. The therapist will then move on to respiration – do you ever have problems breathing or suffer from catarrh or sinusitis? Women will be asked about their menstrual cycle – is it regular, do you get a lot of pain, do you suffer from premenstrual tension or are you going through the menopause? Moving on you will be asked about your circulation – do you often get cold hands or feet, do you know what your blood pressure is?

Having gathered lots of information on your basic bodily functions, the aromatherapist will ask about your general constitution. You will be asked if you get headaches frequently or catch colds more often than most people? Don't be afraid to mention any minor problem you may have at this point. It may seem unrelated but could nevertheless have some bearing on your general well-being.

You will also be asked about your sleeping pattern.
Do you ever have any problems sleeping and if so how
do they affect you? Perhaps you find it hard to get to
sleep, or maybe you wake up in the middle of the night
and can't sleep again. Some people feel they're getting
enough sleep yet still wake up tired next morning. All
this information will be useful when the
aromatherapist chooses a suitable course of treatment.

SOME PEOPLE FEEL THEY'RE GETTING ENOUGH SLEEP
YET STILL WAKE UP TIRED NEXT MORNING..

Stress factors
The case history will now turn to more general
questions about your lifestyle and the particular
pressures you are under.

For many people a major area of stress stems from
the workplace. So many jobs these days force us to
work long hours in a less than ideal environment. We
often think of stress at work being associated with the
high-powered business executive, jet-setting around the

world, but every job has its particular pressures. What about a nurse on night shifts in an understaffed ward or a housing officer in an inner city area? The actual working environment itself can be very stressful – a busy, smoky office with little natural light and full of VDU screens is a good example. How you actually spend your working day is also important – are you on your feet from nine till five, or are you sitting at a desk which is the wrong height for you? Or perhaps the problem is unemployment and all the pressures, both financial and emotional that this can bring. Don't immediately rule out aromatherapy because you can't afford it, ring up the aromatherapist as he or she may be able to offer you a concessionary rate.

For some people, however, stresses stem from home life not the workplace. Being a single parent, running a house as well as having a full-time job can put a lot of additional pressure on us or perhaps you are having problems with teenage children or financial difficulties. Your aromatherapist isn't going to pry into your personal life for the sake of it, but if there is something which is affecting either your physical or emotional state then it is worth mentioning.

Diet and fitness
Our level of fitness will depend on many factors and can have a direct bearing on our well-being. Someone with a sedentary job who takes no form of exercise could run the risk of suffering from obesity or heart problems in later life. The active sportsman on the other hand brings the problems of sports injuries, from torn muscles to injured joints.

The foods we eat often have a direct bearing on our general health, but with some conditions, such as acne and arthritis, our diet is of vital importance in treating the condition. In such cases, the aromatherapist will need to know as much as possible about what you eat and will either offer dietary advice or perhaps refer you to a nutritionist. If you have no specific health complaint, then he or she will just inquire about your awareness of the right foodstuffs to eat and offer advice where appropriate (see Chapter 6).

When we are feeling under pressure many of us reach for some sort of stimulant, be it caffeine, nicotine or alcohol. We may get the lift we need for a short time but the effects soon wear off and we reach again for the coffee jar or cigarette packet. The aromatherapist is likely to ask you how much coffee, tea or alcohol you drink, whether or not you smoke, or if you use any form of drugs. Be honest! The aromatherapist needs to know, and although you will be offered advice, any decision to change these habits will be yours.

Your mind
Finally, the aromatherapist will ask you if there are any emotional problems you wish to talk about. For some people this is just the opportunity they need to talk to someone not involved in their life about a particular difficulty they are having. Sometimes just airing a problem gives you a clearer view to sorting it out. The right essential oils, with their powerful effect on the emotions, may put you in the right frame of mind to do this. On the other hand, if you don't feel comfortable about talking to a 'stranger' on such a personal level then you won't be forced into doing so. Once you've been for several sessions and have built up a relationship with your aromatherapist, then you will be able to talk about emotional matters if you need to.

Body language
In addition to asking lots of questions, the aromatherapist will be picking up lots of non-verbal clues. Body language can give away a lot about your personality, are you sitting in a comfortable relaxed way or are your shoulders hunched and fists clenched in a tense anxious manner? Do you arrive punctually,

looking calm and collected or do you arrive hot and flustered, ten minutes late. Your general appearance can give plenty of information too, as can your complexion and posture. Don't worry about all these clues you are giving away, they too will help the aromatherapist build up a complete picture of you. He or she will then be able to make a choice of essential oils to suit your needs. Some aromatherapists, however, may use other techniques to either find out more information about you or to check the choice of oils.

THE BLEND OF OILS

Having taken a case history and used any diagnostic techniques necessary, the aromatherapist will be able to choose a mixture of oils for you. This will depend on many factors, from physical needs to your emotional state. It may also depend on what you are doing for the rest of the day. If you come before work, then a highly sedating blend would be inappropriate; similarly, stimulating oils would not be a good idea in the evening. If necessary, the aromatherapist will give you some oils to take home and use at night time. You may also be asked to smell the oils that have been chosen before a blend is mixed, or even asked which oils you prefer out of a small selection. If you don't like the blend that has been chosen, you won't enjoy having it massaged into you for an hour! We are also often far more intuitive than we think and are able to pick the oils that our bodies actually need.

THE MASSAGE

The next stage of the session is the massage. At this point you will be given a towel and asked to undress. The aromatherapist may leave the room but more likely he or she will be busy preparing the couch and mixing up your oils. Don't be embarrassed about taking your clothes off – the aromatherapist is quite used to seeing other people's bodies. When you are ready, you will be asked to lie on the couch, where the therapist will cover you with a towel and ask you if you feel comfortable. Don't be afraid to say if you are in any discomfort at any stage during the massage. Some people need support under their backs, others under their knees, if they lie on their back for any length of time.

As the massage begins, the aromatherapist will be looking for any clues as to the state of the muscles. Skin tone, swollen or raised areas, heat or cold can all give clues as to which areas need attention. While working, the aromatherapist will begin to get to know your body and its areas of tension. The best state in which to receive a massage is one of deep relaxation while still retaining an awareness of how the touch of the therapist feels. This is best achieved in silence. For many people this is a relief from the hustle and bustle of the day, but for some, this silence seems uncomfortable at first. Most of us aren't used to being in the company of just one other person without making any form of verbal communication. If this really is a problem the aromatherapist may play some soothing music or perhaps go through some relaxation exercises with you (see Chapter 6).

As described previously, the massage given by the aromatherapist will vary according to your particular needs – slow and soothing for relaxation, brisker if a more invigorating massage is needed. Particular attention will be paid to those parts of the body that need it most. For many people it is their shoulders or lower back, for others it could be work on their sinus points. Being relaxed but aware during a massage can throw up some surprising facts about ourselves. People with very ticklish feet are often amazed when they suddenly find the aromatherapist working on their foot without them dissolving into laughter. Other people find some areas far more sensitive than they imagined. If for some reason it doesn't feel quite right to be touched for example on your stomach, feet or perhaps even knees, then tell the aromatherapist and he or she will leave that area until you feel more comfortable. Massage can be an incredibly powerful therapy. When we hold in our emotions we tense various muscles, locking those emotions in. As the muscles are worked and begin to relax, some people feel these emotions being released. Don't worry if you feel like crying or get angry during a massage, it may be just what you need to do.

OTHER TECHNIQUES USED BY AROMATHERAPISTS

When working on particular clients some

aromatherapists incorporate techniques from other therapies. Below are a few that may be used.

Reflexology

Reflexology or zone therapy has its origins in the ancient Eastern civilizations. The theory behind it is that there are reflexes located in the feet which correspond to every gland, organ and part of the body. If for some reason there is any disorder or blockage in energy flow in some part of the body, then crystalline deposits will be found at the corresponding reflex point on the foot. By feeling for these deposits on the foot the therapist will pick up on problem areas in the body often before the patient knows they exist. This can be a useful diagnostic tool for the aromatherapist, and may help in the choice of oils. Some aromatherapists are also qualified in reflexology, though it is probably unlikely that a therapist will do a full reflexology treatment along with the aromatherapy. Working on troubled reflexes can help rebalance the bodily systems, though it can be quite painful for the first time. Your aromatherapist is most likely to just press the reflex points briefly to check for possible disorders and then begin an aromatherapy massage based on any information uncovered. If appropriate, a separate session concentrating on reflexology only may be suggested.

Touch for health

Applied kinesiology or touch for health, is a system based on the Eastern theory of energy lines or meridians and Western chiropractic knowledge. The theory is that there is a functional connection between specific muscle groups in the body and the energy pathways represented by acupuncture meridians. By testing the strength and tune of various muscle groups, the practitioner is able to detect any imbalances in the energy flow. The meridians correspond to the various organs in the body, such as the heart, bladder, kidneys etc. Touch for health practitioners believe that muscular weakness may be apparent prior to the symptoms of any disorder occurring. So as with reflexology, the therapist is able to detect disease before the patient is actually aware of any symptoms. As before, the aromatherapist may just use touch for health techniques as a diagnostic tool, or may actually work on appropriate points to correct any imbalances.

Touch for health has also proved very useful in detecting food allergies. When the client is exposed to a particular foodstuff to which they have an allergy, a muscle which was previously tested strong will become weak. Some aromatherapists use a similar test with essential oils. Their client holds a bottle of essential oil and a muscle test is performed. If the test is weak, then this oil is not suitable for that person, whereas if it is strong then the body will benefit from its use.

Dowsing
Another method used by some aromatherapists for checking their choice of oils is dowsing. This involves holding a small pendulum over the bottle of oil and asking certain questions, such as 'Is this oil right for this person?' The aromatherapist will then read the movements of the pendulum, which is usually clockwise for yes and anti-clockwise for no. Not all aromatherapists believe in the use of the pendulum in this way, but some do feel it makes a useful check once they have used other information to make a blend.

Shiatsu
Shiatsu is a Japanese style of massage, using finger pressure and the same system of meridians or energy lines as acupuncture. Shiatsu practitioners have undergone a thorough training and study of Oriental philosophies, but some aromatherapists know about the meridians and pressure points and pay attention to

them during the massage. Shiatsu is not a smooth flowing massage in the same way that aromatherapy massage is, and is usually performed fully clothed. Some of the principles, however, can be applied and it can be particularly useful for helping the flow of energy or for drawing attention to an area of the body where the energy is blocked.

The chakras
The idea of the chakras comes from the Eastern philosophy of tantric yoga. They are seven energy centres spaced up the spine from its base to the top of the head. Each is associated with a gland, certain bodily systems, various mental aspects or emotions and one or more colours. The throat chakra, for example, is associated with the thyroid gland, the respiratory system and alimentary canal are seen as its creative centre and its corresponding colours are blue and green. Some aromatherapists will tune into these centres while they work to see if they can detect any energy blocks. This can also be done with a pendulum, as with dowsing for the right essential oil (see page 65). Balancing the energy in the chakras is said to revitalize the body and develop self awareness.

Colour healing
Colour healing dates back to ancient Egypt and is closely connected with the ideas of the chakras (see above). We are attracted to certain colours because they have the same vibrational energy as our auras and are repelled by other colours because of a difference in wavelength. Colour therapists believe that by 'transmitting' appropriate colours via the chakras, they can balance the body, mind and spirit. On a less esoteric level, colour is known to have an effect on our mood and emotions. This is shown in our choice of colours for clothes or the colours we decorate a room with. Indeed, you are unlikely to find an

WE ARE REPELLED BY CERTAIN COLOURS BECAUSE
THEY HAVE A DIFFERENT VIBRATIONAL ENERGY
FROM OUR AURAS...

aromatherapist's room decorated in harsh primary
colours. Pastel colours, healing greens, calming yellows
or warming pinks are much more likely to have been
used.

Spiritual healing
Spiritual healing has existed for thousands of years in
all cultures and takes two forms – laying on of hands
and distant healing where the healing is performed in
the absence of the patient. It is the former that some
aromatherapists use while working. Like other holistic
practitioners, spiritual healers hold the belief that

disease is the result of disharmony from within. They seek to restore balance throughout the whole person including physical, mental and spiritual aspects. Healers see themselves as a link between human life and some greater life force and act as channels for energy to pass from one to the other. If an aromatherapist uses spiritual healing, he or she may or may not tell the client and it will be up to them whether or not they choose to receive this energy, on either a conscious or sub-conscious level.

THE END OF THE SESSION

Whatever techniques the aromatherapist has used, the massage has to come to an end. After finishing the massage the aromatherapist will tell you to relax quietly on the couch for a few minutes. He or she may leave the room to allow you to do this in peace. When you feel ready to move, do so slowly, wriggle your toes and fingers, take some deep breaths and finally have a gentle stretch. If you have been in a state of deep relaxation, you will need time to come back down to earth. When you are ready, you can get off the couch and begin to get dressed.

At this point the aromatherapist will talk to you about further sessions. If there is a particular complaint that needs treating, then you may be asked to come on a weekly basis for the next few weeks. Otherwise it will be up to you when you next visit. It is, however, a good idea to book your next session as you leave, as it is all too easy to let the weeks slip by without realizing it. Building regular aromatherapy sessions into your schedule is a very good way of keeping healthy and coping with the pressures of everyday life.

Payment for the session will usually be made at the reception desk in a clinic or health centre or directly to the therapist if he or she works at home. If you would

like regular sessions but genuinely cannot afford it,
then do ask about the possibility of a concessionary
rate for a course of treatment.

The next chapter deals with ways of using
aromatherapy at home between sessions and also other
techniques to help cope with stress and aid relaxation.

6.
CONTINUING
TREATMENT

At the end of the first session, the aromatherapist will have built up quite a comprehensive picture of you, both from the case history and the massage. However this is rarely complete. There may be various gaps in information, problems you don't feel comfortable talking about initially. Sometimes the real root of a problem will only reveal itself after several sessions, once a rapport has built up between therapist and client. This enables the aromatherapist to choose the right oils for you. The same oils may be used over a period of time or they may vary as your condition or needs change. You will usually be asked at the end of a session to be conscious of how you feel in the next few hours or the next day, even the next week. Your feedback will also help to find the right blend of oils.

The aromatherapist will discuss with you when to come back and how regularly you would like to come for sessions. How you can help yourself at home in the meantime will also be discussed. Aromatherapy is a holistic treatment and your therapist will try to offer all the help he or she can, not just in using essential oils but in giving advice about many other things. The aromatherapist will often be able to give you addresses of other alternative practitioners, yoga groups, self-help groups, counsellors and anyone who will be able to help you make any change you might wish to make in your lifestyle. Of course, it will be entirely up to you whether or not to take this advice. The aromatherapist is there to use oils and massage and to provide information and advice, but it is the patient who ultimately heals him or herself. Sometimes a client isn't ready to make changes in their lifestyle, and may or may not continue with the aromatherapy sessions. Many people on the other hand find themselves with a new awareness about their minds and bodies and become more conscious about what they eat, how they react to stress and how they relate to other people and their environment. Aromatherapy sessions can just be the start of many changes, and below are some ways that work in the treatment room can be carried on at home.

USING ESSENTIAL OILS AT HOME

The aromatherapist will often give you some essential oils to take away and use at home. These may be for you to use in the bath, to massage into your body or to use for inhalations. The essential oils will usually be given to you ready diluted with a label saying what they are and how to use them.

If you become interested in aromatherapy and the effects of the essential oils, you may want to begin experimenting on your own at home. This is fine as long as you use the oils with care, asking advice from your aromatherapist or by using a good book. Though essential oils are safe and free from side-effects when used by a qualified therapist, they are very concentrated substances and need to be used in the correct way. Below are some brief guidelines about using the essential oils and some suggestions about the ones that will be most useful to you at home.

YOU MAY WANT TO BEGIN EXPERIMENTING ON YOUR OWN AT HOME...

Methods of application

Details of how essential oils are administered are given in Chapter 3, but here is an idea of dilutions of the oils suitable for home use. Some oils can cause irritation to sensitive skins (these are indicated below) so begin with half the normal dilution stated and increase to normal if no reaction is experienced. The same applies when using oils for elderly people and children. It is possible to use essential oils for babies and very young children, though only in very weak dilutions – I would advise just using the mildest of oils, camomile and lavender, and not exceeding a dilution of one drop of essential oil to 1 teaspoon of carrier oil. If using the oils in a child's or elderly person's bath always dilute them in base oil first and agitate the water well to disperse the oil.

Baths – Add 4 to 8 drops of neat oil to the surface of the water just before getting into the bath and mix the water to spread the oil. Alternatively mix up a bottle of bath oil by using any vegetable-based carrier oil (see page 40) and adding up to 50 drops of one or more essential oils to 50ml of base oil. Always store this bath oil in a dark glass bottle and if you are going to keep it for more than a month add a teaspoon (5ml) of wheatgerm oil to stop it going rancid. Use 1 teaspoon for each bath and to get full benefit from the oils, soak in the bath for twenty minutes.

Massage oils – Make up as for bath oil, but only use 25 drops of essential oil per 50ml of base oil (see page 40). Store, as for bath oil, in a dark glass bottle. Alternatively make up as required, using 6 drops of essential oil to 1 tablespoon of carrier oil.

Vaporization – Place 5 to 8 drops of essential oil on a source of heat (see page 36, Chapter 3 for possibilities).

Compresses – Use 6 drops of essential oil to ½ pint of hot or cold water. Put a flannel or a piece of lint on top of the water, wring out and apply to the affected area. Leave until the compress has returned to body temperature (for cold water) or has cooled down (for hot water), then reapply as above. Repeat three to six times or until pain has eased.

Inhalations – Begin with 1 drop of essential oil to a drop of near boiling water. Increase the number of drops if necessary up to a maximum of 6 drops. If you don't have the facilities to do this, put a couple of drops of oil onto a handkerchief or inhale directly from the bottle.

Internal – Although some books on aromatherapy recommend taking essential oils on a spoon of honey, in honey water or on a sugar cube, I strongly advise against it. If you are interested in taking the oils as an internal medicine, then find an aromatherapist with a medical/clinical background who will make up the oils for you.

Ten essential oils for home use

Ask a group of aromatherapists to choose the ten essential oils they use most often and the lists might differ considerably. Each therapist has his or her own favourites, though I doubt if lavender would be missing from any of the lists. Below is my list of ten. I've tried to pick a variety of aromas from floral to exotic, citrus and herby and a combination of sedatives and stimulants. The list of further reading on pages 101–102 suggests some of the many books available at the moment, which deal with the oils in more depth.

Lavender – A great all-round oil with a familiar fragrance, it is often described as 'balancing' in its nature. It is good first aid oil, useful for burns and cuts, headaches, colds, 'flu and sinusitis, as well as for general aches and pains. It is helpful for cases of anxiety and depression and also for insomnia. A lavender bath is a perfect end to the day, easing a tired body and mind at once. Lavender also blends well with most other oils.

Rosemary – Having slept well after a lavender bath, get yourself going next morning with a stimulating rosemary one. Rosemary helps the memory and concentration and eases general debility and fatigue. It is a useful tonic for the heart, liver and gall bladder and makes a good inhalant for respiratory problems. As an oil which is useful to ease muscles after physical exertion, try combining it with lavender for an after sports rub. It is also warming when used for rheumatic pain and has a history of being a good hair tonic. It can cause irritation to sensitive skin and should be avoided by pregnant women and epileptics.

Bergamot – This refreshing citrus oil comes from the fruit of the bergamia tree which grows mainly in southern Italy. It is a wonderfully uplifting oil, useful for many forms of anxiety and depression. It is particularly useful for urinary infections such as cystitis and also for skin care, especially for oily skin and acne. If you like Earl Grey tea (which is China tea with added oil of bergamot) you are sure to like this essence. This oil makes the skin more sensitive to the sun's rays so don't use it before going out in strong sunlight.

Geranium – There is some dispute between authorities on essential oils as to whether this light, floral oil is sedative or stimulating. It does have a pronounced effect on the nervous system, though different people tend to react to it in different ways. It is useful for skin conditions, being both antiseptic and anti-inflammatory and has a balancing effect on the hormonal system. It is good for poor elimination and conditions such as cellulitis.

Camomile – Camomile is a calming and soothing oil, which is useful for many children's ailments. It is a mild oil and in very weak dilutions (though never to be taken internally) it can be very helpful for treating teething pains and soothing fractious toddlers. It contains a powerful anti-inflammatory constituent and is also analgesic, so is useful for aches and pains, from backache, headaches and ear ache to stomach ache and period pains. On an emotional level, its action mirrors that on a physical plane, that is it is good for states of restlessness and nervous irritability.

Juniper – Juniper has been known since ancient times for its antiseptic properties. It is a great cleanser, useful for helping the body eliminate toxins and therefore indicated for the treatment of arthritis, gout and rheumatism, as well as conditions such as water retention and obesity and also some forms of eczema. It is also helpful for clearing the mind, especially if problems stem from contact with other people.

Basil – I am including basil in the list, primarily for its use as a nerve tonic. It is used for clearing the head and is great when you need to use your intellectual faculties. It can help with indecisiveness and with certain cases of anxiety and depression. Though it is a stimulant, I find it useful mixed with lavender in cases of insomnia, where sleeplessness is caused by thoughts churning through the mind. It is good for respiratory problems and for sluggish or congested skin conditions. Use in weak dilution as it can cause irritation.

Eucalyptus – Eucalyptus is probably best known for its affinity with the respiratory tract, where its antiseptic, expectorant and antispasmodic actions are helpful in relieving conditions from sinusitis to bronchitis. It has a cooling effect on the body, so is good for feverish conditions. It can also be used for muscular aches and pains and rheumatoid arthritis. As an antiviral agent, it can be used in epidemics of 'flu or measles to help stop the spread of infection.

Sandalwood – Sandalwood is my favourite choice from the exotics for its woody, sensuous smell and indeed it is renowned as a potent aphrodisiac. It is highly sedative and can be useful for depression of the tense, uptight kind. In skin care its action tends to be balancing and it has benefits for dry, dehydrated skin and oily skin alike. It also has an affinity with the respiratory tract. It is useful for bronchitis sufferers to use as a chest rub at night as it eases the congestion, while at the same time by helping with the anxiety caused by breathlessness, it helps promote sleep.

Rose – Though rose is extremely expensive, it is a beautiful floral oil which is seen as being particularly feminine. It is a useful antidepressant, especially when

ROSE IS AN
APHRODISIAC

the depression is linked in some way to female sexuality. It is an aphrodisiac, useful for frigidity and impotence and is useful for coping with grief. For skin care, it is helpful for ageing and sensitive skins. Though costly it needs only to be used sparingly.

Carrier Oils
Any vegetable oil can be used as a base for massage. This does *not* include baby oil, which is mineral based and therefore will not penetrate the skin. The following are my favourites.

Grapeseed – This is a light, easily absorbed, inexpensive oil which is good for full body massage. It is completely odourless, making it an ideal base for essential oils.

Wheatgerm – This rich oil is high in vitamin E, which is good for any skin condition, from dry skin to healing scars and blemishes. Use up to 25 per cent combined with another base oil.

MASSAGE

Self-massage
Massaging yourself is not the same as being massaged by someone else, as you are the one doing all the work. Therefore it is not especially relaxing but it still has many positive benefits, including improving circulation, toning muscles and tissues and increasing self-awareness. Many of the books around at the moment (see Further Reading on pages 101–102 for a few ideas) have a self-massage sequence in them, but you can be quite intuitive and listen to what your body needs. Only a few basic rules apply. One is in general to work towards the heart, that is up the legs and arms

and secondly be gentle with the delicate skin of the face, especially around the eyes. The hardest part to massage, and unfortunately the part most often needing attention, is the back. Try using your fists, but if you really feel your muscles need working try one of those long handled massage rollers that are popular at the moment.

Do-in is the self-massage form of the Japanese massage, shiatsu (see pages 65–6). It tends to be a fairly vigorous form of massage, which can be quite invigorating and energizing. If you are lucky you may be able to find a do-in class, otherwise some of the shiatsu books now on the market have sequences to follow.

Massaging others

Giving a massage can be as pleasurable as receiving one. Having massage from a professional therapist is good training for massaging others. Again there are many good books around but don't try to be too ambitious at first. So long as you avoid too deep pressure and don't work on the spine itself you won't do any harm. Begin by using long smooth strokes and as you become more confident try some different ones. Don't worry about not getting it 'right', as long as it feels good to the receiver then it is fine. Make sure your partner feels warm and comfortable and try to tune into their needs. It can be a rewarding experience for you, as well as a relaxing one for your partner. If you become really interested, many massage practitioners run workshops, sometimes through local education authorities so they are quite inexpensive.

BACH FLOWER REMEDIES

The Bach flower remedies comprise a system of 38 remedies prepared from the flowers of wild plants, trees and bushes. They are not used directly for physical complaints but rather for the mental state behind them. The belief is that not only do negative states of mind, such as fear, hopelessness and irritability, hinder recovery from illness but they are in fact the primary cause of ill health and disease. Dr Edward Bach was an Welsh doctor, who gave up his practice in 1930 to develop his series of remedies which work on a very subtle level, allowing patients to find peace and harmony and thereby heal themselves. The difference between flower remedies and essential oils is that essential oils work on physical, mental and emotional levels simultaneously. Some aromatherapists use the remedies to back up their treatment with essential oils and give clients a bottle of prepared remedy to take home. However the instructions and literature on the Bach remedies are self-explanatory and they are thus ideal for self-help. There are some good books around and many people find that reading about the principles of the 38 remedies helps them discover personality traits or negative states of mind.

The remedies are roughly seen as being of two different groups. The first group of 'type' remedies are said to define the basic fundamental nature of a person. Most people can identify with a 'type' remedy which will have both positive and negative states. If you have a tendency to display the negative traits of a certain remedy, taking it will help you move back to its positive state. Other remedies are seen as 'helpers' which are used to back-up 'type' remedies or to give help at particular moments in time. For example, agrimony, a 'type' remedy, is for people who tend to hide worries behind a brave face, whereas walnut is a 'helper' used for times of change or transition, be it puberty, marriage or a new job.

The remedies are available from some chemists and many healthfood shops. They come with a free leaflet, giving instructions on use and a brief description of each remedy. You may want to start just with this and

81

move on to more detailed books later. The remedies are completely safe, with no side-effects. You cannot choose the 'wrong' remedy, if your body does not need one of the ones you take it simply will not use it.

NUTRITION

'You are what you eat' is a phrase that is widely used these days, yet one that many people pay little attention to. Though there is a general trend towards healthier eating, our supermarket shelves are still stocked with sugar, salt and additive laden foods with little nutritional value. The aromatherapist will probably ask about your diet during the case history and in some cases it may be suggested that you make radical changes in your diet to supplement your treatment.

Conditions which are aggravated by eating the wrong foods include arthritis, acne, catarrh and many stress related problems. A lot of work has been done on diet and arthritis sufferers and there are some excellent books around full of case histories to show that dietary change really can help. The diets may be strict and you need to be committed to follow them, but the results can be dramatic. Teenagers with acne have notoriously bad diets, snacking on crisps, sweets and fizzy drinks. They may find it hard, but a change in diet is really essential. Catarrh sufferers will benefit from cutting down on mucous forming foods such as dairy and wheat products and for all stress related conditions a reduction in the intake of stimulants, tea, coffee, alcohol and some food additives, can be important. Even if you have no particular health problems at present, a good diet is a good form of preventative healthcare.

When we talk about changing our diet, most people think only about the things they will have to cut out. I prefer to concentrate on all the new things they have never thought of trying. So you have to cut down on tea and coffee, but there is a huge range of herbal teas to experiment with these days. Instead of the staple bread, rice and pasta, try grains like millet, buckwheat, bulgar and couscous. Meat intake can be reduced by increasing the amount of pulses, nuts and seeds we eat. The basic rules for good nutrition are as follows. Try to avoid pre-packaged foods as much as possible, replacing them with fresh foods. If you do eat canned or packet food, choose ones without additives, sugar or salt. Eat plenty of fresh fruit and vegetables, organically grown is best but not practical for most people – wash it well instead. If you eat meat, cut right down on red meat, replacing it with lean white meat, or better still eat more fish. Vegetarianism is fine, but do not go overboard on the dairy produce. Try to keep your diet as varied as possible with plenty of different grains, pulses, nuts and seeds. Coffee is best avoided, but if you cannot give it up, cut down to a couple of cups a day and keep tea intake down as well. If you still want to drink alcohol, stick to wine and try diluting it with spring water.

Once you have discovered how good it feels to eat well, you might want to take it a stage further and try the occasional fast. This does not mean cutting out all food but could instead involve just eating fruit and vegetables for a few days or just drinking grape juice and spring water. On page 100 I have given the addresses of two organizations that produce books and leaflets on diets but if you are in any doubt or if you have any medical condition, check with your doctor first before fasting.

Nutritional supplements

In theory we should be able to get all our requirements for vitamins and minerals from our food. In practice few of us have a perfect diet and environmental factors, such as pollution, increase our need for vitamins. If you feel as though you need to take some supplements but are overwhelmed by the array of bottles and packets in the healthfood shop, ask your aromatherapist for some advice. He or she may be able to suggest a reputable brand of multi-vitamins/minerals (some are laden with sugar and additives) or, if you need more specific advice, recommend a nutritional consultant. Many conditions these days are being treated by high dosage supplementation, though this should always be undertaken under the guidance of a trained nutritionist.

RELAXATION

For most of us, relaxation is sitting in front of the television, reading a good book, taking a long walk or enjoying a game of squash. Though these are all good forms of stress release or of switching off from the daily grind of work, the emphasis is still on *doing* something

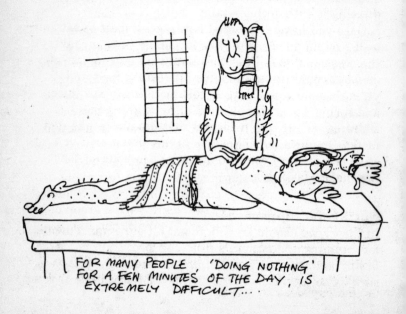

FOR MANY PEOPLE, 'DOING NOTHING' FOR A FEW MINUTES OF THE DAY, IS EXTREMELY DIFFICULT....

rather than simply *being*. We live in a world which puts ever increasing importance on making things happen, rather than letting things happen, and for many people 'doing nothing' even for a few minutes a day is extremely difficult. Having a massage is a very good opportunity to lie for an hour and let go, putting your trust in the therapist. Taking this one step further is to try to build a relaxation spot into your daily routine. There are many ways of doing this, some incorporating movement such as yoga and t'ai chi, others involving techniques such as autosuggestion and visualization. Then there are various forms of meditation. It may take a while to find something that fits your own lifestyle, but there is no doubt that relaxing for a short time each day can have many positive effects on health and well-being.

Yoga

Yoga is no longer seen as something 'cranky' that is practised by the hippy brigade, but has become enormously popular as men and women of all ages and walks of life have come to appreciate the benefits of this ancient Eastern technique. The most common form of yoga taught and practised in Britain is hatha yoga. This involves a system of stretching postures or *asanas* which exercise all parts of the body, keeping muscles well-tuned and stimulating the circulation. In addition to this you will learn breathing exercises, or pranayama, which are wonderfully calming and revitalizing, and some form of meditation technique. You can teach yourself yoga from a book, though most people prefer to join a class and learn with a group of others from a qualified teacher. You will then find it easier to practise at home. Most adult education centres run yoga evening classes or maybe a local community centre runs drop-in classes where you turn up and pay week by week.

T'ai chi chuan

Though not as well known as yoga at present, t'ai chi is becoming increasingly popular. Its roots are in ancient China and it can be used as a form of self-defence, though in the West it is most often used as a form of exercise to relax the mind and body. When practising t'ai chi you learn what is known as a form, which for beginners consists of about 50 different postures linked together by slow, gentle, flowing movements. Like yoga, it exercises muscles, improves circulation and balances energy levels. Again, it can be practised by people of any age. All you need is a small space and you can even practise in the office at lunchtime for ten minutes or so. It is important though to find a good teacher to learn the basics from, and then you can practise daily.

Autosuggestion and autogenic training

Autosuggestion is something we do subconsciously all the time. We talk ourselves into feeling warm because the sun is out, even though there might be a cold breeze. Using this idea we can consciously talk ourselves into a state of relaxation by sitting or lying quietly and repeating slowly to ourselves words like 're-lax' or 'he-avy'.

A more sophisticated version of this technique is known as autogenic training or AT and is a method of deep relaxation and greater self-awareness. It can be practised in either a sitting or a lying position and involves persuading various parts of the body to generate their own sensations. You begin by turning your attention to one part of the body and saying, for example, 'my right arm is heavy', repeating this until your arm really does feel heavy and then moving on to another part of your body. You then progress to thinking yourself warm. Next you 'think' your heart beat calm and register your breathing as slow and deep, your abdomen (solar plexus) warm, and your forehead cool. At the end of the exercise you return to the world with the phrase 'I am refreshed and alert'.

The exercises should involve an attitude of 'passive concentration' where you say the phrase then observe what sensations or emotions you become aware of. Some people find this system quite hard to use on their own at first and so use a taped sequence, either made themselves or bought ready-made. Though obviously using a tape is not quite the same as autosuggestion, as you cannot work at your own pace, it is still a very useful relaxation aid.

Progressive relaxation

This is a simpler technique than AT (see above) and can be practised easily at home with no tuition necessary. It involves putting a group of muscles into a state of tension, then letting go and feeling the different sensation. You usually begin at your toes, working right up your face, finally trying to clear your mind of all thoughts. Again you can use a tape (or a friend) to talk you through the sequence.

Meditation

Many people think of meditation as something practised by Buddhist monks or various religious sects. This is not so and the many forms of meditation can be extremely beneficial for overcoming anxiety, releasing tension and refreshing the mind. When practised, meditation can produce what is known as a *hypometabolic* (very relaxed) state of body, where your heart beat slows down, blood pressure drops and breathing becomes slower and shallower. Your mind switches to a state of 'relaxed wakefulness'. This state can be more restful and constructive than sleep. Meditation can either be 'taught' as in transcendental meditation (TM) or learnt at home following a few simple guidelines. In TM you will go to an introductory talk, then have several individual sessions with an instructor where you will be given your own personal mantra or chant, to use when you meditate. While some people find that they need to learn the technique in order to have the will power to practise at home, others find they can manage quite well by following these four basic conditions. First is finding a quiet place where you will not be disturbed, second is sitting or lying in a relaxed position. You then need to focus on a constant mental stimulus. This could be auditory, a sound or a word or phrase repeated either silently or

FOR MEDITATION FIND A QUIET PLACE WHERE YOU WON'T BE DISTURBED....

out loud, or a visual image, either an actual object or a mental picture. Finally, you need to adopt a passive attitude, that is not working too hard at achieving anything, and if thoughts come in, just note them and return to the technique. Meditation like this is known as concentration or contemplation and is the type most commonly practised in the West. At much deeper levels of meditation the practitioner will completely forget the self and leave behind both body and mind as he or she transcends to a higher state of being.

7.
THE FUTURE
OF
AROMATHERAPY

Interest in aromatherapy has grown enormously in the last ten years and as this trend continues, there are likely to be many changes and developments. Below is a brief discussion of how aromatherapy may progress in the future.

BEAUTY PRODUCTS AND PERFUMES

Many manufacturers of cosmetics and even some of the large fragrance houses have jumped on the aromatherapy bandwagon and are marketing products containing essential oils. Professionals in the field of aromatherapy are in two minds as to the merits of this. Some feel that it is trivializing the more serious side of aromatherapy, while others think that by drawing the public's attention to aromatherapy in this form, some people are more likely to explore the topic further. Sometimes the so-called aromatherapy oils on sale are synthetic and not natural oils, though it is often difficult for an untrained nose to tell the difference. If you are interested in aromatherapy beauty products, some of the suppliers' addresses, who deal with mail order, are given on pages 98–100.

MEDICAL (OR CLINICAL) AROMATHERAPY

Turning to the other end of the spectrum, there is a growing interest in the medical uses of aromatherapy. At present there are very few practitioners in Britain who use essential oils to treat infectious or organic diseases. Those who do are either herbalists or orthodox doctors, both of whom are legally able to diagnose disease and prescribe medication. The story is slightly different in France, where most people have followed the same path as Dr Jean Valnet and his way of using essential oils (see page 12). It is now possible to undertake courses in scientific aromatherapy in Britain but there is some debate as to whether it is safe to teach non-medically qualified people about the medical uses of essential oils. Perhaps one hope for the future would be to have an aromatherapy course similar to that taken by medical herbalists, covering all aspects of aromatherapy including clinical diagnosis as well as holistic pratice.

HOLISTIC AROMATHERAPY

This book has covered the use of aromatherapy in what could be termed as its holistic form – looking at the whole person and treating the underlying causes of disease. It often deals with psychosomatic illness, but considering that even the BMA agrees that a high proportion of disease could be classified as such, then it is no less important than so-called clinical aromatherapy (see above). Though the distinction between the different strands of aromatherapy can be useful, there is no reason why practitioners cannot use all of them together.

FUTURE LEGISLATION

Within the next few years, probably by 1990, there may be new legislation in Britain which will affect many practitioners of alternative medicine. There is already in progress a review of the 1968 Medicines Act, and licences for many herbal medicines have been revoked. At present essential oils are classified under three categories – foodstuffs and flavourings, cosmetic ingredients and pharmaceutical products – and so do not need licences. However, with the increasing emphasis on medical aromatherapy, it is, in theory, possible for the government to insist on licensing essential oils. It is generally thought that this would be too difficult a project to undertake, considering the many active constituents of essential oils. The other possibility is that there may be new laws defining who should be classified as an alternative practitioner. The French are pressing for all EEC countries to conform with them and only allow people who are medically qualified to practise any other form of therapy. This would have dramatic consequences for alternative therapy in this country and many people believe it would be impossible to implement. How, for example, would masseurs using essential oils, or spiritual healers be classified?

The British government has stated that it will only negotiate on these topics with representative national bodies, which for aromatherapists would be the IFA (International Federation of Aromatherapists). The Natural Medicines Society has been set up to rally support from manufacturers of natural products, practitioners and the general public.

PURITY OF ESSENTIAL OILS

There has been much concern recently about the purity of essential oils available in Britain. Towards the end of 1987, 16 of the major essential oil companies in Britain, along with three university research departments formed the Essential Oil Trade Association. Among the aims of the association were education and having a guarantee of purity. They hope to be able to issue what they call the *aromark*, to essential oils which have reached a defined grade of purity. This mark would be recognized by the trade consumer council and standards officers and would be a great help for practitioners and consumers alike.

AROMATHERAPY IN THE COMMUNITY

At present, aromatherapy is largely in the domain of the middle classes who can afford private sessions. There are, however, people who are trying to take aromatherapy to a wider public. I worked for a time as

an aromatherapist in a swimming pool, employed by
Hackney Council in London's East End. Others have
worked in hospices and hospitals with old people and
handicapped children. All this work needs to be
continued and expanded in order to dispel the myth
that aromatherapy is exclusively for the well-off.
Grants or funding by local authorities or other sectors
of society are desperately needed to help further these
aims.

Interest in all forms of alternative medicine, including
aromatherapy, is certainly on the increase and
hopefully this will continue for years to come. There is
a lot of pressure for scientific research to be conducted,
to support some of the claims made by alternative
practitioners. While this may give the alternative
medical world more credibility with the orthodox
medical profession, we should not belittle the benefits
many patients have received purely from the caring,
holistic approach of alternative therapists in all fields.
After all, if by some means we manage to give our
clients the ability to heal themselves, the method we
use is surely secondary.

USEFUL ADDRESSES

PROFESSIONAL ORGANIZATIONS

International Federation of Aromatherapists (IFA)
46 Dalkeith Road
West Dulwich
London SE21 8LS

Send an sae for a list of accredited training schools or a
list of IFA members in your area. You may also join
the IFA as a friend, no specific qualifications required.

Association of Tisserand Aromatherapists
31 Craven Street
London WC2

TRAINING SCHOOLS

There are many colleges teaching aromatherapy,
ranging from those offering 2-year courses to others
offering much shorter diploma courses for those with
knowledge of either massage or another form of
healthcare. More details are obtainable from the IFA
(see above). Here are some of the more well-known
ones:

London School of Aromatherapy
PO Box 780
London NE6 5EQ

9-12 months home tuition with weekend practical
workshops. Send 25 pence stamps for prospectus.

The Tisserand Aromatherapy Institute
3 Shirley Street
Hove
East Sussex BN3 3WJ

Shirley Price Aromatherapy
Wesley House
Stockwell Head
Hinkley
Leicestershire LE10 1RD

ESSENTIAL OIL SUPPLIERS

For mail order send sae for price list.

Lifeworks
Centre for Natural Health Care and Remedies
11 Southampton Road
London NW5 4JS

Shop, mail order and clinic.

Essentially Oils Limited
6 Stoughton Avenue
Leicester LE2 2DR

Mail order. Also carry own range of natural body care
products.

Norman and Germaine Rich
2 Coral Gardens
London SW14 7DG

Mail order for professional therapists.

Body Treats Limited
15 Approach Road
Raynes Park
London SW20 8BA

Mail order.

Butterbur and Sage Limited
Greenfield House
21 Avenue Road
Southall
Middlesex UB1 3B1

Mail order.

Aromatherapy Supplies Limited
52 St Aubyns Road
Fishergate
Brighton
Sussex BN4 1PE

Supply professional therapists with Tisserand pure essential oils, which are also widely available from healthfood shops.

Shirley Price Aromatherapy Limited
Wesley House
Stockwell House
Hinkley
Leicestershire LE10 1RD

Suppliers of essential oils and range of natural skin care products. Mail order.

Neals Yard Apothecary
2 Neals Yard
Covent Garden
London WC2
Tel: 01-379 7222

Shop and mail order.

Fleur (Aromatherapy Skin Care and Aromatic Treats)
8 Baden Road
London N8 7RJ

The Body Shop – many outlets throughout Britain.

Sells essential oils and blends, diluted ready for use.

NUTRITION

You can join either of the following two organizations or send for their book lists.

Institute of Optimum Nutrition
3 Jerdan Place
London SW6 1BE
Tel: 01-385 7984

Also runs various workshops on nutrition.

Green Farm Nutrition Centre
Burwash Common
East Sussex TN19 7LX

Runs courses, sells mail order supplements and has an off-print service with articles covering areas of nutrition and health.

FURTHER READING

GENERAL

The Art of Aromatherapy, Robert Tisserand
(C W Daniel)

An essential book for professionals and lay people
alike. Background information on history and use of
essential oils, plus comprehensive profiles of 24
commonly used oils.

The Practice of Aromatherapy, Dr Jean Valnet
(C W Daniel)

Written by one of the pioneers of aromatherapy and
translated into English. This is the most detailed work
available here on essential oils. The approach is
clinical.

Practical Aromatherapy, Shirley Price (Thorsons)

A good beginners guide for using aromatherapy for
self-help at home. Sections on massage and reflexology,
a therapeutic cross reference section and plenty of
recipes.

Aromatherapy, Judith Jackson (Dorling Kindersley)

Useful guide for those wishing to experiment with aromatherapy massage. Includes a good self-massage sequence.

Aromatherapy, an A to Z, Patricia Davies (C W Daniel)

Comprehensive guide to essential oils and their uses, plus many other related topics.

MASSAGE

The Massage Book, George Downing (Penguin)

Written in 1974, this book really describes the Esalen method of massage. It gives thorough instructions for a full body massage.

Massage for Healing and Relaxation, Carola Beresford Cooke (Arlington Books)

This is a book of a television series. Includes massage for different groups of people, from the elderly to children and babies. Includes some shiatsu and a self-massage sequence.

The Book of Massage, various authors (Ebury Press)

Comprehensive guide covering massage, shiatsu and reflexology. Plenty of illustrations, step by step instructions and authoritative advice.

BACH FLOWER REMEDIES

Bach Flower Therapy, Mechfild Scheffer (Thorsons)

How to use the 38 remedies, plus a full profile of each.

Also any of the guides produced by:
The Bach Centre
Mount Vennon
Sotwell
Wallingford
Oxon OX10 0PZ

JOURNALS

Aromatherapy Quarterly
c/o 46 Westminster Crescent
Hastings
East Sussex TN34 2AW

International Journal of Aromatherapy
3 Shirley Street
Hove
East Sussex BN3 3WJ

INDEX

ABOUT THE AUTHOR

GILL MARTIN is a practising aromatherapist and a
member of the International Federation of Aromatherapists. She first became interested in alternative medicine at university, but only began her aromatherapy
training after working as a chef in a vegetarian
restaurant and in food retailing.

She has since worked both in private practice and as
an aromatherapist at a local council swimming pool.
Currently she combines her private practice with
working for The Body Shop.

More books from Optima

ALTERNATIVE HEALTH SERIES

ACUPUNCTURE

Dr Michael Nightingale

Acupuncture is a traditional Chinese therapy which usually (but not always) uses needles to stimulate the body's own energy and so bring healing. The author is a practising acupuncturist well aware of the particular concerns of first time patients.

ALEXANDER TECHNIQUE

Chris Stevens

Alexander Technique is a way of becoming more aware of balance, posture and movement in everyday activities. It can not only cure various complaints related to posture, such as backache, but teaches people to use their body more effectively and reduces stress.

MEDITATION
Erica Smith and *Nicholas Wilks*

Meditation is a state of inner stillness which has been
cultivated by mystics for thousands of years. The main
reason for its recent popularity is that regular practice has
been found to improve mental and physical health,
largely due to its role in alleviating stress.

HYPNOSIS
Ursula Markham

Hypnosis has a remarkable record of curing a wide range
of ills. Ursula Markham, a practising hypnotherapist,
explains how, by releasing inner tensions, hypnosis can
help people to heal themselves.

All Optima books are available at your bookshop or newsagent, or can be ordered from the following address:
   Little, Brown and Company (UK) Limited,
   P.O. Box 11,
   Falmouth,
   Cornwall TR10 9EN.

Alternatively you may fax your order to the above address. Fax No. 0326 376423.

Payments can be made as follows: cheque, postal order (payable to Little, Brown and Company) or by credit cards, Visa/Access. Do not send cash or currency. UK customers and B.F.P.O. please allow £1.00 for postage and packing for the first book, plus 50p for the second book, plus 30p for each additional book up to a maximum charge of £3.00 (7 books plus).

Overseas customers including Ireland, please allow £2.00 for the first book plus £1.00 for the second book, plus 50p for each additional book.

NAME (Block Letters) ....

....

ADDRESS ....

....

....

☐ I enclose my remittance for _____

☐ I wish to pay by Access/Visa Card

Number | | | | | | | | | | | | | | | |

Card Expiry Date | | | | |